NOT YET A JEDI

Not Yet a Jedi © 2022
Partridge Boswell
All Rights Reserved

No part of this book may be used or reproduced in any manner whatssoever without permission except in the case of brief quotations embodied in critical essays or reviews.

Attention schools and businesses; for discounted copies on large orders please contact the publisher directly.

Kallisto Gaia Press Inc.
1801 E. 51st Street
Suite 365-246
Austin TX 78723
info@kallistogaiapress.org
(254) 654-7205

Cover Design: Mary Day Long
Cover Photo: Patrick Page

ISBN: 978-1-952224-26-3

NOT YET A JEDI

POEMS

PARTRIDGE BOSWELL

TABLE OF CONTENTS

Are We Here?	1
Pop a Wheelie	2
Upon Mistaking "pressure" for "pleasure" in a Poem by Anne Carson	3
Champs-Élysées	4
Ode to Westminster Street	6
Ode to Apollo	8
Hungry Freaks Daddy	9
Upon Hearing Amy Winehouse at St. James' Church in Dingle	11
Thinking of Klimt's *Stoclet Frieze* during a Two-hour Delay	12
Late Shift at the Foxfire Diner	13
Ode to the Umbrella	14
Ode to Invasive Species	15
The Chosen	17
West of Troy	18
Prayer	19
Strike Anywhere	20
Ode to an Afterthought	22
Haibun to a Lost Cousin	26
Three Thousand Miles	27
Last Night in America	28
Not Yet a Jedi	29
Parting Shot	30
SparkNotes	32
Acknowledgements	35

for **Sarah**

—*Livicated to Ralph Angel* (1951-2020)

I'm working on a song
that wakes men up
and lets children sleep

—From *Cançao Amiga*
by Carlos Drummond de Andrade

Are We Here?

Unschooling *The Hustle* in your basement, a bellbottom
       universe flares. Your mirror ball world begins to spin
when you ask Laura O'Riordan to the church dance.

Night's diorama dilates, displacing tender shards.
       Your black-lit heart blooms luminous in the blue dark.
No one tells you this will make you stronger. No one says

have fun proving relativity wrong. *Your kids will actually*
       do better without you. Who *says* that? Some geek charting
another numb notch on the spectrum—must not hail from

around here, no one local gathers rice from the wedding
       to boil for the wake. Sparks of a mirrored orb you unjive
and scatter again. No one tests the telemetry from mother

to child, the milk of a blind eye. A ride on Space Mountain
       eternally hurtling through a wormhole of hairy celerity lasts
a few seconds before "reality" abandons quotations again.

You glue a fractured mosaic, a prism to gyre and gimble
       on curfew's scrim—grooving the parish hall in a holy
kaleidoscope of disco-ball-stained-glass. Waves of moog

crash over folded tables and chairs stacked to one side.
       Your wallflower universe too weird not to be trusted, too
wondrous not to don shades and boogie the velvet night away.

Pop a Wheelie

From oil-dank bowels of a nightmare garage you ride
        beknighted, Saturday morning's acolyte, sleep-dazed
but aright, straight for the ramp you built last night

in the driveway in homage to the great adrenaline-hazed
        Evel Knievel—archetype for every dangerboy and bone-
headed troglodyte bent on a bright schematic vying to break

more bones than the Guinness World Record flying prone
        over cars buses lions fountains sharks canyons rattlesnakes—
before the neighborhood wakes. Topping the slope you rev

your banana bike and pedal hard on the approach past
        a hushed gang of squirrels and robins holding their breath
half-hoping this levitation will and won't be your last.

Did he always wear stars and stripes? Was his helmet
        screwed on tight? Will his next attempt be televised
if he succeeds and fails yet again to reach the light?

Devil dared and fair-warned, you rocket as advertised
        off a wood plank sailing headlong over fame's coliseum—
into your first kiss and beer and Eucharist, your first dorm

room farewell and first rock concert at the Orpheum,
        your body's first chemistry experiments and first storm
of contrite indignation shadowing your first arrest,

your firstborn's silence like a warm ghost, your island
        that formed in a widening ocean when your first
Greyhound pulled away from the curb taking a friend-

more-than-a-friend, inevitable as the first long gaze
        that followed soaring through every stunt since,
angling for the abyss, realizing too late your trajectory's

off by an inch and this is going to hurt. You brace
        yourself for that embrace.

Upon Mistaking "pressure" for "pleasure" in a Poem by Anne Carson

There is a certain kind of pressure in humans to take whatever is most beloved by / them and smash it.

We thought of it as play but in truth
our parents had no clue where we were
or what we were doing. One path led
to another. What little bread we had
we ate en route and left no crumbs
so even birds would starve. Riprap
uneven and lethal, ties too narrow
or wide, never matching our stride.
Tracks so long their chiasmus singing
mercy in both directions. What did we
care if opposites were true? We knew
where we were going and there was no
going through; the fear shunting us here
always only boxcars boxcars boxcars
never people. We thought less and less.
At first we only wanted to see what would
happen to the penny, then everyone had
their own penny minted with their own
likeness. Soon we were so rich everyone
wanted to see what would happen. It was
like a sickness, but only like. Everyone
liked their own likeness. Everyone liked
owning their own likeness. Until all that
kept us sane was a promise of disaster.
We knelt and placed our ears to the rail,
waited for the iron's faint ringing to grow
real and unstoppable as a comet they said
would never hit us though it would take
one to prove a penny is still worth saving.

Champs-Élysées

> *I think it is terrible and disgusting how everyone has treated Lance Armstrong, especially after what he achieved… When I was on drugs, I couldn't even find my bike.*
> —Willie Nelson

Every action, Krishna enjoins Arjuna, *is surrounded by defects*
       as fire is surrounded by smoke, i.e. it's fine to appear at the starting
line drunk or smoke a pack of Gauloises from Évian to Parc des Princes

as Pietro Vittorino did in the golden days, winning three stages
       and the mountains jersey including victories atop the mythic airless
heights of Alpe d'Huez and Mont Ventoux. And who didn't idolize

sprinting ace Jacques d'Argnac, who swore the bottle of absinthe
       he guzzled as pious as a postulant before every stage
gave his legs the rapid-fire reflex of a Citroën's pistons?

Each glory-bent masochist has his system, his magic beans,
       his shoulder chip and secret asterisk to fetishize a grail and
separate him from the blindered peloton rolling through

countryside otherwise too sublime not to gasp and pause
       indefinitely lingering along a line of plane trees bordering
endless lavender, a trellis sea or the amaranthine café in

a cobbled Alpen town whose name forever eludes you.
       The maillot jaune pacing ego's deep addiction, beaten daily
down and left for dead in a roadside ditch, revived each dawn

with a lacerating whiff of mortal salts—an unfazed Saint George
       enhanced by poison, swords, and molten lead, at last beheaded
where we find him kneeling in that massive pentimento of passion

hanging in his eponymous cathedral in Piran: every onlooker,
       executioner and friend regarding him with shame, pity,
envy, remorse or some variation on the human course

of devotion. Too late to grab the artist's brush and revise
       the drama of legend, too late to hoist another dragon slayer
shoulder high, his eyes alone fixed upon the angels—hovering

with uncertain wings unable to discern a distinction between
        victor and victim, fame and infamy, a fabled Bordeaux and sour
grapes—circling like vultures above him in a perfect summer sky.

Ode to Westminster Street

—after cummings and Spinoza

We do not know what a body can do...
how when she crossed the street

asking you for a dollar so she could
get something to eat, you fished in your

pocket and peeled a twenty from a sheaf
of bills saying: *This is all I have.*

Bless you. You have a good night she said
and took your hand in both of hers before

drifting off into an unconscious city, the wind
eddying in doorways of vacant buildings.

We do not know the bottom of surrender,
swirling our fingers in an oily reflection:

hope and courage are rolls of unused tickets
bequeathed to wide-eyed children as we leave

the fair. She wore a dress striped black and white
as if darkness were imprisoned, or light—impossible

to tell which caused effect, effect or cause, her body
and mind knifing one kinesis, her burning thought

and infinite blood inhabiting the same sword of illusion
as she crossed the empty street. We were dreaming

with our eyes open, confabulating our nimble
inadequate ideas while strolling after sushi

back to campus. Her arms were bare, the air
still warm enough to empathize without caring

though the season was turning, about to betray itself:
first, the leaves, then snow, giving for once a soft

white damn. Then birds vanishing into clouds,
taking our naïve assumptions with them.

Ode to Apollo

Which astronaut performed a Eucharist on the moon?
          our daughter asks glued to the trivia app on her phone.
We have no clue, but now imagine the body and blood

consecrating that airless weightless dust, the wine
          curling gracefully up from the bottle into the cup,
desiccated lilies rising from a tranquil sea of rock

and lambs gamboling in craters with dogs named
          Laika and Pluto, grazing the barren landscape
of a brain that quips: "If English was good enough

for Jesus, it's good enough for me," noshing lumpy
          gray matter of a colonized cosmology, the sacred
universe and profane university interchangeable as

two astronauts who in their levity stood and looked
          back over their shoulders at the lush blue-green fluke
of us swaddled in mist floating utterly bereft in that

impossible abyss, as one of them reached for a six
          iron from his bag. The kind of god who can swap out
Delos and Delphi for Houston and Cape Canaveral,

a laurel for thorns, the roar of his four-horse chariot
          setting fire to the sky. His bow and lyre harmonizing
a medicinal music of capricious arrows—confusing isms

and schisms, fusing a man with a mission. The kind of man
          who walks for miles and miles and miles without leaving
a single footprint scribbled on its watery surface.

Hungry Freaks Daddy

Slept as sound as a bug in a barrel of morphine.—Thomas Edison

Moon floats over Fatick tonight, useless and
        serene as the abandoned village in your heart.
Edison invented More's beacon so fireflies

could just have sex, angst-free from having
        to enchant us. So we could all be just friends
and stage less credible facsimiles of our dreams.

The blank headstone of Moon's vacancy sign
        winks through wax myrtle. By silent consensus
we agree not to visit the inlet of sleeping sea cows.

Edison invented the phonograph so his dog could
        hear his owner's voice and cock his head. Moon
invented a way of looking at Sun minus dark

glasses. Those who are tone deaf to Earth
        can at least pretend to hear a dog's music. Edison
wore a bow tie every day his whole lumen long;

he wouldn't be led astray by the leash of another
        man's notion. He wore one tarpon fishing with his
son Charles, whom they called Charles. Sadly,

it did not light up or spin; that would be another
        man's invention. His son's mother Mina planted
moonlight in a garden with its own reflecting pool

reinventing stars and stones and Moon's own
        stellar invention, framed by the leaves' consensus
of shadow. Edison invented fear of everything beyond

the pale throw of incandescence, as if the gap between
        ignorance and unknowing were bridgeable, as if mystery
were a mystery to be solved, if only we could stay up

late enough. Edison invented the toothpick so we
        could prop our eyes open while waiting for the whelk
and periwinkle of the impossible to wash up onto

the strand of what we didn't know we needed.
        Music invents a village with no electricity
or running water where every child laughs and

dances, absent the least idea of one man's ability
        to complicate simplicity. Edison invented one
thousand-ninety-one other ways to approximate

waking dreams, endlessly waking from his penitent
        sleep of reason, abandoning approximation for closer
approximations, layering failure upon failure to *forestall*

the rising tide of hungry freaks, daddy—according to
        the opening track of *Freak Out!* by the Mothers of
Invention, consistently voted one of the top hundred

albums ever made, thanks again to Edison whose own
        mother yanked him out of school and taught him herself
after a teacher called her son *addled*, Edison who invented

Heaven so we wouldn't have to fly or remove our shoes
        or weather the wand and cavity check, leaving automated
profiling at the gate for another man to patent, which is bound

to happen now that it's not just an idea floating around
        but an actual fly on paper, buzzing like a wire now
in a dim corner of the room, hot to admonish: *Stop*

waiting for another mother's son or daughter to dream
        your dream *for* you of a more blindingly fundamental
filament that burns the unlit backdoor of bigotry's retina

to dust. Wake not, refreshed from your spotless power
        nap to resume wherever the utilitarian bulb of your head
happened to switch-off, only to be drowned by the wave

of another man's ocean. Wake, not because you can,
        but must.

Upon Hearing Amy Winehouse at St. James' Church in Dingle

Grief without song could be any stone chapel built of loss
packed with aging villagers lulled reticent as rue
by a rote bell's tongue, hemmed by iron gates and a yew
tree lurking mirthlessly beside a burial ground where moss-

patinaed saints and earth angels gather round relic icons
of threadbare hand-me-down faith. You sit/kneel/stand on
your misericord, an eaten Job in the organ belly's drone,
sorting your parents' hoarded aggregate—clothes pawn

and charity shops won't take, sewing kits, boxes of old
Polaroids of anonymous sepia-people you wouldn't be here
without, file drawers of past taxes, uniforms from the war,
wedding dress, unworn shoes unfit for a holy soul…

—and that's just the tip, to say nil of unspeakable sins
in attic and basement. Macular shorebirds scan whitecaps
for questions the mind's eye can alight: dim synapse
of a candlelit nave, musty kneelers, a deacon's

chair from Suriname. Grief without song is wasted pain.
According to patron James, *faith in works*—in real acts
of creation—amplifies our part in salvation's soundtrack
louder than wafers, wine or words of mumbled expiation

dissolved on penitent tongues. In your rusted anechoic
husk, your veins blood-thrum a rushing river-hymn,
an electric fence of nerves ticking in your cerebellum—
until silence clears its throat…and from her first chthonic

tremolo it comes as no shock: how from Galway to Summerhill
churches are being repurposed as concert halls by clergy who swear
love's lost call note still lingers, runic under the moored murmur
of all those services you sat unmoved through, the supernal

flatulence of organ bellows at last revised in fidelity rare
as a black velvet angel with spindly legs and mental hair,
her aqueous blues beguiling as the B-side of prayer
beside an ocean we couldn't hear but always knew was there.

Thinking of Klimt's *Stoclet Frieze* during a Two-hour Delay

> *I think I'm on the planet Mars!*
>   —Belgian architect upon touring Palais Stoclet

The tree glows leafless but alive, its spiraling tendrils
    frozen as it twines from floor to ceiling of the Palais
dining room. A degree warmer and this would all be

melted and we'd be on our way to school. A degree
    colder and the curling branches would not be crazed,
the roads lightly dusted with snow, not glazed with ice.

A degree or two and we'd be happy and warm inside
    and out, not shivering before the storm speculating
if forecasts are real or fake, straddling the threshold

in liminal jaundiced light, Expectation's gaze fixed
    on Fulfillment's embrace. Life/death heaven/earth
intertwine suspended in space. A fist-sized hole

in the wall would be a hole, an absence of plaster
    and paint, not the grief you walk around all day
and at night fall into. You'd be sitting at the table

wielding a Wiener Werkstätte spoon over a bowl
    of warm fiddlehead soup, eating your meal in peace
while trees are growing over you instead of cities.

Late Shift at the Foxfire Diner

The porch light fails and you never replace it.
        Drive the last dirt mile with headlights dimmed.
Ramble grass logging roads by memory and feel

what it is to be animal again—reinhabiting
        hunger and hunt, skulking low to the ground
in deep woods on a dark night to steal a glimpse

of her cold atavistic fire seeping between
        damp moss and leaves. Her bioluminescence
less coy and naive, brighter since she ditched

her bombazine, no more wan crescent cloaked
        under the same old lie—mythic enough now
to seduce a moth or read herstory by, raped

but this time willing to testify—unchained
        from the fisted melody she called love,
the narcissist who picked her up late if at all.

86'd with Elvis, *God speed,* and pickups.
        Ditto stereotypes truer than old gum stuck
to a booth's underside. Glued to your counter stool

nursing a bottomless cup—convinced you got
        what it takes, as if you're the blue plate special
& worth the wait. As if patience alone could save her

as she offers you a free slice of day old cherry pie,
        the jukebox in your head cueing your favorite
rhapsody at B2, biding your time till vinyl's back in style,

idling for the last booth to leave, for her to remove
        her apron and slip her coat from its hook at the end
of an endless shift, though you haven't even made

eye contact yet, only smudged the same cup with
        fingerprints—your shared dreams unattainable
and real as ridges and whorled seas of the moon.

Ode to the Umbrella

> *Upon receiving an email "Student Walkout Planned" to "send postcards…to representatives on the topic of school safety"*

Bobbies never carry one though it rains and rains on that calm
dignified island. Here we wear them strapped to our waists and
chests like feelings without fabric. Who needs words anyway
to describe madness—so old fashioned!—when action figures
so prominently in our fiction? We must live on too wide an island
where thunder heads can roll for miles and never hit their targets
until they do. Too free to be held and yet, we need something
to hold onto. On that mild island where it almost never snows
they're brandishing bumbershoots common as colds, so common
their hands are evolving into handles, their hair into triggers and
minds into canopies of dread, their fingers into ferrules aimed
at whatever may be falling from the unsaid. Assembly is simple,
instructions easy to follow as precipitation when words fail
and they will; we drag out the brolly we carry unconcealed
at our side or the five stacked in the cab rack of our pickup we
peer through like fence slats at Antietam. Chip chip cheerio,
here have a go: they're insanely easy to deploy, a child can do it
and has, so easy to just grab when you hear the day's forecast
calling for cloudbursts inside nightclubs churches elementary
schools supermarkets government buildings—a real gully-washer
could take you by surprise even if your mood toward humans
isn't graying and skies are perfectly blue and children are playing.
The more we see them, the more we'll trust their usefulness
like a shoe that keeps our foot dry from puddles of rain or
blood or what-have-you. The right to bare arms is a sacred
and personal choice that begins in the womb. If I want to wear
a tank top in January like it's the Fourth of July why shouldn't I?
Besides, I'll have my trusty bumbershoot at my side no matter the weather—
a lover I can love so freely and deeply I can't even sleep without her
cold hard steel packed beneath my pillow. But here I've made fun
of a name anyone from that island would never call them, just as
Dunblane was the first and only soulless wordless total eclipse
of every daughter and son, the only one anyone needed to trigger
their hearts' consensus of common sense and put it plainly on paper—
an act so easy even a child knows how to pick up a pen and erase a gun.

Ode to Invasive Species

You'll need a cement jaw, gloves of thick raw-
        hide and bombproof canvas pants, a sharp spade
maybe a pick to pry soil loose around the base,

a mild day after a night of rain to soften their
        resolve, an intolerant epithet or two to remind
them who owns the sun and rain, the nutrient-

rich loam here merely on loan. Loppers alone
        won't do. You'll need to grab low, yank and
wrench maybe even dig before roots unscrew

their tapered lengths from rhizomatic depths
        lukewarm & dark as the womb of a surrogate
who consents to birth but not to motherhood.

You'll need a uniformed conservation corps
        of eager unformed youth who won't connect
the green sweat of just another summer job

with an angry mob's generic objective, who
        will hear in their names only the thorn in buck-
thorn, the strife in loosestrife, the knot in knot-

weed, the suck in honeysuckle, the Russian
        in Russian olive, the false in false indigo, the
heave in tree of heaven. Access to a 24/7 news

channel might help, but since your genocide's
        low tech, all you'll really need is the hook of
a melody's veiled invective, catchy as Sweet

Home Alabama where kudzu runs more rampant
        than whatever genus crooned the land back to
sleep after the Centennial Exposition where

the miraculous new plant from Japan was first
        introduced along with the telephone and type-
writer and their unborn progeny of devices

that are now more endemic than air.

The Chosen

Gypsy moths choose their favorite tree while
neighbors just as lush and green escape unscathed.
Deciding which deciduous victim is more messianic
or a better host, only moths can track such traits.

I watched my dad remove the gray ghost of each colony
spreading on the mountain ash he planted beside the house—
flaming bunches of bright orange berries glowing against
the white-washed garage—prune their gauzy clouds

of writhing larvae into a Maxwell House can, pour gasoline
and torch them in the driveway in roughly the spot where
he rolled out the Weber grill summer Saturdays to conduct
his Viking funeral for cows pigs and chickens before

we ate them. This way, each meal became a burnt offering
and wake, every animal thanked in our closest simulation
of the sun that sustained us even on bad days, promising
its return. The only black skin I saw growing up on

that street were my own hands fondling charcoal
before he lit a fire. But this poem isn't about race or
vegetarianism, or coffee brands, or even a genocide
that occurred in a patch of side yard, on the corner

of a street named for a bird, at the edge of a town
clinging to the tip of a glacier-gouged lake. It's about
the migrant farm camp tucked in an apple orchard
at the end of our road—low gray barracks' sheet

metal roofs moaning a dusky tannin-sweet song.
When new construction bumped up against the farm
one night the camp burned to the ground—a heap
of charred bunks and twisted metal. Families gone

like smoke found another crop in another valley
to the north, leaving someone else to resolve
in the nick of an eye and twist of wrist
which would ripen or be lost to windfall.

West of Troy

...it's snowing hard on the road to Buffalo, flakes so dense
        lights and wipers make little difference. *Maybe we
should turn around* he concedes. Fine by me. I'm not exactly
        thrilled to be taking SATs in a strange empty high school
tomorrow morning. But I say nothing. Better to just get it
        over & done, cut the BS so we can get on with learning.

Never have sex with someone unless you love her

he says apropos of snow, knowing he has me pinned between
        an ice-slick Scylla and Charybdis of dodgy conditions and
the test I'm about to take. As if maybe I'll have a multiple choice
        question on that tomorrow and have to pencil in a tiny oval.

And did you love them...the ones before Mom?

I ask, innocent as, well, a child, knowing he married late.
        Why yes, I suppose I did... So says the man who:

    A. visited Circe's island no less than seven times
    (by my mother's count) before I left high school

    B. my mother never once asked for a divorce

    C. hasn't ever mentioned to me his other son

    D. assumes love for me will be a woman

    E. embodies none and all of the above

You are so beautiful to me Joe Cocker rasps tenderly
        through a static squall to the wipers' futile metronome—
and for the moment I feel safe, his loving hands white-
        knuckling the wheel. What I don't know can't hurt me
though we're inside already moving through something
        both perilous and incomprehensibly beautiful that wants
to bury us alive for the plows to find come morning when
        as far as we can see, the world will be an empty oval
                filled with nothing but snow.

Prayer

> *One cannot transcend trauma. Trauma is trapped and clings to that which happened. We live not after trauma, but in its aftermath.*
> —Carolyn Forché

I shouldn't tell you these things, they'll only traumatize you. But how else
        disarm the daily harm of putting oneself in others' harm's way? And how
can one not ask, after the girl was hospitalized yesterday, her condition

uncertain? Brain damage. Intensive care. Not the sort of thing you want
        to hear right now, but I'm telling you. In her home there's television and
substances, uses and abuses. Did I mention she's two? I shouldn't tell you

but who among the fallen oligarchies would listen without disdain? Home
        is an abattoir of second-hand toys and stuffed animals—a crib-sized play-
penitentiary, walls without window or door, womb without ceiling or floor.

One cannot transcend one's past, only bleed in its aftermath. She sees me
        in daycare and lights up, reaches when I bend and scoop her in my arms,
clings tight to me like the oak tree that was safety when we played tag

with friends in the yard, and says *Mamma* in my ear. How can one not hear?
        Iron skillet, shotgun, pillow, syringe—substances and their uses. It's hard to
be precise when one has seen the apartment. A grave at least would have

flowers. I shouldn't tell one who is equally vulnerable and powerless;
        that would be mocking disability, misfortune, hardship. But how else
endure the offering? Isn't that empathy without action? (only to one who

cares) Isn't that karma? (only to one who believes) While you were out
        looking for god, I signed some papers, tried to put wheels in motion
that were already spinning. I'll shut up now. Thanks for listening.

Strike Anywhere

It starts innocently enough, waiting for dinner to live up
        to the boast of its aroma: *Teleportation. Invisibility cloak.*
The ability to fly! our young waxwing all but shouts.

I'd have speed so fast I could turn back the clock his brother sallies,
        syncing his mind's meteoric veerings, now that he's off Ritalin.
What about you? they ask. *What superpower would* you *have?*

Russia. I tease. But they don't laugh and leave me crouched
        in a fetal ball beneath my school desk, ears cupped to muffle
a siren's wail. *Thumbs, I'd settle for thumbs.* But they don't want

to hear from Darwin or Nietzsche—they want my own real POV,
        an honest answer on a serious subject. I'm fumbling around
in a box of blue tip matches the gods let us steal as a consolation

for celestial passion. The tip flares and instantly the boys are
        my age, and I'm trying to parse for them wisdom from lies.
What would do the most good and least harm? Saying sorry

for all I've felt and haven't said? Would I want to die again
        and again, and come back each time more grateful than
the last? Didn't Hendrix say: *When the power of love*

overcomes the love of power then the world will know peace?
        Or was that Lennon? Either way, it was definitely Yoko who
said: *A dream you dream alone is only a dream. A dream you*

dream together is reality. I could be Orpheus, able to warm
        the coldest stone with a few notes, to lift the lowest among us
or sing anyone down off their loftiest ledge with a hit so heart-

rending it reminds us we were loved once and will love again—
        a music so strong it sucks the in- out of inhumanity, voicing what
we're capable of, drowning out disappointment's self-fulfilling

loop of canned Muzak…But *which* Orpheus? The one before
        or after he finds the minor key? Or after he's torn apart?
I strike another match and light a candle. They're hungry

so we tuck in around the table, drawn by the surging urge
        Icarus felt as he soared toward the light that conjured us,
our capes and masks draped over the backs of our chairs.

Here we are, this is us. The tender peppery leaves of rocket,
        croutons crispy yet soft. I know but don't say what power
I *wouldn't* want: *to see into their futures.* Our hands are open

and empty; our plan—a scrap of light we keep in our pocket.
        Which superpower? Here's a hint: *there's only one.*

Ode to an Afterthought

> *I was late for this, late for that,*
> *late for the love of my life*—Lumineers

Copper light leaks from a cracked dome   minutes of this morning's
    meeting dissipate in whispered wraiths of convened clouds
clearing the docket for ghosts to come as they come   you're someone other
    than you sparking a bombless fuse homeward   gliding through stealth
grace happily gathering shards of patient subterfuge like that monk in Montreal
    who tried to scam you   a gold card membership in the club of
        enlightenment instead of just asking

    the how and what about.

for a handout   asterisk to the everyday miracle of driving around town
    windows rolled down in mild disbelief   a suicide therapist
crawling inside a client's empty   cocoon to find a small yellow butterfly
    flitting in the abyss of a September afternoon embalmed in what
        must surely be the last eighty degree day before

    the who and why and what the fuck.

everything heads south bleeding mercury   retreating rebel soldiers thirsting
    for a front porch tune marching   daily from errand to appointment
diffused in the patina of a million inconsequentials dying into another endless
    gestation   another frost's first refusal
        naked stubble of field corn reborn

    the two seconds it *took to assess her situation.*
        the last-ditch universe and no one else.

on hunters' faces beginning to unveil   their prehistoric camouflage
    the season's osmotic evasion enchanting your aversion to the light
industrial strip at this hour bumper-to-bumper creeping   through endless inter-
    changes past faceless malls   steering you instead
        the back way home along suburban streets

    the how did I fail her and myself.

another new recruit of the slow commuter movement ceding all
        to the luster of rationed light   slanting into tinged

leaves bungalows mottled yards milling children after school
        abandoning the rote route you listen for one   oxbowed note floating
            south out of town settling for stop signs timed to bittersweet
                lines of Lumineers' *Cleopatra*

    the easy bag of donuts and ATM cash you could hand her.

on the radio hearing in one voice   all the loveless
        who've never wasted or waded in the hand-dug well that turns waste-
land to oasis or who have and couldn't taste it afraid of a little drowning or
        convinced something cleaner would come along   a million & one empty-
            sleeved excuses deceits & self-exemptions digressing until
                the possibility of giving

        the how hard can it be. the day spinning its wheels.
            the traffic to wade and waste your amygdalae on.

yourself over is a wallaby   foraging on the shores of Lake Disappointment
        …when you arrive at a nondescript intersection where ranch homes
unconsciously segue   into box stores car dealerships & fast food:
      a stop sign where the steady flow of impulse pauses no
            longer than the rolling innuendo of

    the season in no hurry to revoke or redeem itself.

a comma before one last zig   zag into the main artery
        nothing could trigger warn or brace you for her standing
pigeon-toed on the corner   her face about to melt *verging on*
    cliché   but these are real tears real   glasses and pigtails
                reminding you of the girl next door who used

    the why not resist and defy. the *inconvenience*.

to babysit you   no older than your own daughter who's learning
        how to drive her abject eyes adrift in a middle distance some   where
between the drivers' gazes she can't quite   bring herself to meet and the sign
        she's holding: *Pregnant and Homeless. / Will accept*
            help of any kind.

      the questions you're cool with asking
           so long as you're not asked to live them.

…and here's your day in a cracked nut   shell unable to look away /
     looking away to negotiate one more turn on the lam along a fugitive
detour of conformity   sparing yourself the impatience of fellow cells
     who it turns out   weren't opting for a slower more
          meditative route home only a faster way out
              of town and are now

     the drive home unable to abandon
         the home growing inside her.

cursing her under their breath for making them   feel   some   thing
    lone casualties of another's courage   flowing down the next
block past the convenience-store/slash/Dunkin-Donuts-drive-thru-you-pull-into
      and drown   in a cloudburst from lucid sky you risk
     a glance in   your mirror: there she is
        still on the corner facing

    the every intention you have of returning
        to that corner tomorrow. the stopping and
          getting out. the music con/fusing.

that impossible metronome a steady stream of cars   pausing because
    it has to the gamut of mercies shirking past in momentary
blindness from *What about that empty guestroom?* to *If she's so destitute
    where did she get the cardboard and Sharpie?*   *If she has the where
      withal and gumption to make*   *herself the poster
       child of self-pity, surely*

    the rude score of horns and jeers. the no
       matter what route you take she'll always
          be standing there on your way home.

she's clever enough to imagine another way out?   *Hey kid!* the driver of
    a pickup shouts *Try reading*   *a little Nietzsche!* but this after
noon there's no other way in   or out only her life the way she's
    lived it   *Silly me* you blame it on the song the angle
      of the sun you get your shit to

       the kind of help a river carries.
            the monk who ferries you across.

gether and rejoin the main drag   leaving the scene of a crimeless
      crime merging behind an older car of a certain make & model
retrieving to mind uninvited: the first time you   tried on those
      three naked words *I*   *love*   *you* when she looked
          straight through you and said   *Now why*
                 did you have to go and ruin
                     a perfectly good thing

     the feeling before. the feeling after.
          the lowering light igniting the river.
               the one to cross the one you're in.

Haibun to a Lost Cousin

> *Here,*
> *I'm here—*
> *The snow falling*
>   —Issa

Between the retaining wall and new suicide fence
they've installed on the bridge over the gorge
after the smattering began to multiply who

placed their shoes neatly on the sidewalk
by the railing only high enough to keep
young children from falling

        lies an empty field
filled with snow not far from the hospital where
your older cousin would go for treatment.

He visits your house only once to say hey in the hall
with his mom who brings him as if to prove the boy
we never talk about actually exists, stays no more

than a haiku—a first and last impression
not long enough to remove his shoes to wade
across your mother's immaculate floors.

To you he looks happy, not sick or troubled or high
but you're just a kid and what do kids know aside
from swings and an empty cicada husk clinging

to an apple branch? His head's a bit shaggy
but long hair means something then. He's smiling
and you're a little scared; the fence they erected

is high but you can still see through it.

On the other side
   lies a field of falling snow.
You try to smile back.

Three Thousand Miles

We didn't choose to live here but decided to make the most of it.
        Then the cows lolloped home and the ballyhoo ensued. Aisling brought her tree frogs in a shoe box. We gathered around and wanted to touch

but hesitated. *They're not poisonous* she insisted, but we had our doubts.
        Especially about the blue and yellow one that reminded me of a drag queen at a stock car race. Their toe suckers reminded me of ET. A

National Guard jet flew low and sonic over the house, shaking the walls,
        the table, the box, the trees outside. Reminding me of the pilot's steady hands on the controls, the people sitting around their living rooms with

nothing to do, all the clandestine armed conflicts in other hemispheres
        they'll never hear about, all the devils to be served and which kind of barista are you: counter-love or copy speech? The frogs shook like jello.

Otherwise, after the plane vamoosed they didn't move much. Not like
        the leapers in Calaveras County. I chalked their lethargy up to being three thousand miles from home with a foot of snow outside. Reminding

me of songs by the Pretenders, Proclaimers and Louis MacNeice proposing
        that snow makes *even the Future / Seem long ago*, which reminded at least one of us how desperately before Aisling arrived we were trying to invent

a war without anyone dying. *They're poikilotherms* she said *they adapt to*
        whatever climate they're in. Maybe I'm not convinced, but those frogs sure were something to look at, even if they weren't real.

Last Night in America

Even the moon knew the party was a tick past last call
        whenever like clockwork your class Einstein
would crank Springsteen to twelve and proceed

to strip to his skivvies in the front yard of whoever's house,
        regardless who might witness the shitfaced blaze of a jackass-
savant who evidently needed a break from tests and term papers.

As night's blue blackened, he'd slip the cassette from his
        pocket into the stereo like an engagement ring dredged from
the bottom of a blue-collar benzene river in Jersey intended for

the finger of the girl-next-door who always lived
        somewhere else. And for a song or two he'd make
the river do what he wanted it to—writhing and lurching,

windmilling the night with his air guitar, belting out the Boss
        verbatim into his shoe, building his ablution to a crescendo
of beer-graced longing born not to run but to burn his idol-

soul in a red light pole dance at the Stone Pony.
        Goading partyers and gods alike (not least himself)
to heal this holy night, bellowing off-key a lyric beyond

hope of finding love in this broken bottle speed trap town
        while friends hooted & howled and girls ducked inside
horrified by their own curiosity. Sometimes parents

or even police would arrive with a blanket…
        and by his third or fourth encore you knew the way
to Thunder Road and Jungleland as well as the back

of his mojo hand, knew the party's hungry heart would
        give out any minute now, bleeding into streets
going nowhere with no place left to hide.

Not Yet a Jedi

So certain are you and yet still work to be done there is.
Yet thanked your mother for being her son you've not.
Not yet a wookiee found you can trust nor yet a Millennial
Falcon fired up nor the leap to lightspeed made nor your

light saber switched to stun. Not yet a star discovered
that bled or crushed not anyone from the inside-out,
not yet your father's darkness forced onto the couch.
Not yet the workforce vetted for likeminded freedom

fighters, traitors and insurgents. Not yet Foo Fighters
heard live nor moshed the whites of their eyes to see.
Luminous beings are we, not yet baptized by the taste
of mama's manna fried. Not yet teleported from the

Starship Enterprise. Not yet crisscross applesauce
singing small children songs in a circle set. Not yet
old enough to vote or emerge from your hole your
shadow to behold, yet a world without money or

mirrors hung you've not, nor from your arms the glue
and feathers washed. Especially to you the second law
of thermodynamics applies, yet accepted you have not.
When 900 years you reach, look this good, you will not.

Parting Shot

> *...it is always very dark here in the future*
> —Matthew Zapruder

Let me be clear I hear a lot lately, presumably since we've never
        been more muddled than this moonless midnight at high noon,
never more nebulous than this starless Chautauqua. Let my clarity

be a din of synthesis on this golden smoldering dawn, now and always
        both our anniversary and what would have been George Floyd's 48th
birthday. I raise a cracked glass to the unlikelihood of us—thinking of

a forefather whose name I ride, invoking him in our fight to exorcise
        our unending inbred depravations and shortcomings, our enslavement
to the past, confounded how in a hundred-sixty years nothing's changed...

how, wounded in the trenches at Cold Harbor, he was sent home
        to Potsdam, his war ended, surrendered to the hope that maybe just maybe
brothers won't have to fight and die again for the sake of their brothers

and sisters, that dark as the future is, a union will prevail, annealed by our
        differences—like those my bride's relation, a sharpshooter from Carolina,
carried with him: his skillet for a pillow, his ten pound Parrot rifle he fired

at the edge of a peach orchard while comrades retreated, making his
        the last shot fired at Gettysburg. No one seems to know or care if
that late bullet found its mark. Did he miss the memo or intend it as

a harbinger, reckoning his side had borne the worst of the carnage
        (though clearly both sides bled) and let one last curse fly anyway
out of spite? Could he or my family's counterpart dream the true

cost of evolution would be so far off the suggested retail price?
        At Fredericksburg the Rebs were so cold and broken they "stuffed"
dead Yanks for clothes and left their bodies naked on the fairgrounds.

How long is the shelf life of shame? What happens when ghosts don't die
        and their necromancers emerge from hiding to parade behind the lie?
The dead bury what kin they can while the living clean their guns

and finger their scars, stashing rancor's sores in borrowed uniforms
        to fester long after the sun and its regiment of shadows moves on
across empty fields, along dirt roads of redemption toward home.

Bookended by darkness, we drink to the day that learns its past
        well enough to bury it for good, trusting Matthew knew what
Jesus meant when he said: *The last shall be first and first last.*

                —14 October 2021

SparkNotes

> *I think youngsters need to start thinking about what kind of world they're going to leave for Keith Richards and me.*—Willie Nelson

We wouldn't be here if it weren't for our children
        who decided to use this evening's sporting event
as a pretext to show how they really feel

getting everyone to light the wax taper of a thin
        paper lantern in an empty field behind the school
on a bitter January night—a local gesture

intended to draw attention to bullying here at home,
        though who isn't thinking globally too as we huddle
in tight circles to shield a candle flame, urging the wax tablet

to catch and fill the bladder of each luminescent jellyfish
        with enough heat to defy the numbing air? Surely there was
a teacher or administrator behind all this? But no, we're told

the children thought of it all by themselves, they even called
        the fire department and secured a permit. While politicians
are plotting the next deception, our sons and daughters

are igniting the next generation and the next,
        measuring the distance between the world as it is
and the one they envision, seeing lucidly in the task at hand

the hand guided by the head guided by the heart
        determined not to outsmart itself this time,
the gloveless hand focused, despite this being

a good night for frostbite, on spreading what little light it can,
        despite the futility and forever of it, solidarity ephemeral
as paper fire sucked up a flue into infinite ash.

None of which will make tonight's headlines beside
        a darkened tower in the city of light, but as we watch them
multiply and soar beyond our sight, and so become stars themselves—

each the gift of a victim's spirit, each a sacrifice no one demanded—
    their pale hope continues to rise higher and higher into the icy void ringing long after paper and fire have burned themselves out.

Grateful acknowledgement is made to the editors, readers and judges of the following publications and venues in which versions of poems first appeared:

Cede Poetry: "Ode to Apollo"
december: "The Chosen"
Fish Anthology: "Last Night in America"
Gemini Magazine: "Ode to the Umbrella"
Green Mountains Review: "Ode to Westminster Street"
Forklift, Ohio: "Hungry Freaks Daddy"
Fungi: "Late Shift at the Foxfire Diner"
Hotel Amerika: "Are We Here?" and "Not Yet a Jedi"
IthacaLit: "Ode to an Afterthought"
Poem of the Moment: "Upon Mistaking 'pressure' for 'pleasure' in a Poem by Anne Carson"
Prairie Schooner: "Prayer"
Poetry: "Upon Hearing Amy Winehouse at St. James' Church in Dingle"
Poetry Ireland Review: "Ode to Invasive Species"
Red Wheelbarrow: "Pop a Wheelie"
Reed Magazine: "Strike Anywhere"
Salmagundi: "Upon Mistaking 'pressure' for 'pleasure' in a Poem by Anne Carson"
Smartish Pace: "Haibun to a Lost Cousin"
Southword: "Three Thousand Miles"
SurVision: "Thinking of Klimt's Stoclet Frieze during a Two-Hour Delay"
The Gettysburg Review: "Champs-Élysées"

"Pop a Wheelie" was selected by Ellen Bass for the 2017 Red Wheelbarrow Poetry Prize
"Upon Hearing Amy Winehouse at St. James' Church in Dingle" was selected for the 2020 Telluride Institute Fischer Prize (finalist)
"Ode to the Umbrella" was selected for the 2019 Bray Festival and Gemini Open Poetry Prizes
"Thinking of Klimt's *Stoclet Frieze* during a Two-Hour Delay" was shortlisted by Brenda Hillman for the 2019 Robinson Jeffers Tor House Poetry Prize.
"Last Night in America" was shortlisted by Ellen Bass for the 2018 Fish Poetry Prize.
"The Chosen" was shortlisted by Amy Nezhukumatathil for the 2020 Jeff Marks Memorial Poetry Prize.

My deep thanks to Tatooine & back to the fine folks at Kallisto Gaia, especially Tony Burnett for his close attention in shepherding these words into your hands and to Wendy Barnes for taking a shine to them… and of course, to Master Yoda. Love to my family, friends, teachers and co-creators for their ongoing affirmation, encouragement and inspiration…

    …and to you, for taking the leap of reading these poems.

www.ingramcontent.com/pod-product-compliance
Lightning Source LLC
Chambersburg PA
CBHW022059120526
44592CB00033B/410